香港國際詩歌之夜 *2011*
INTERNATIONAL POETRY NIGHTS IN HONG KONG

編輯 Editors
方梓勳 Gilbert C. F. Fong
陳嘉恩 Shelby K. Y. Chan
柯夏智 Lucas Klein
何潔賢 Amy Ho Kit Yin
北島 Bei Dao

維瓦克・那拉揚南
Vivek Narayanan

目錄 Contents

A Meeting with the Senior Poet Who Hated Me

Last night I used up in a dream all
        that I had to give
                reading out my collected works in

some grimly renovated tube-lit hall.

It took a while, and when it was done

—without a word, without applause—each member
of the audience stood up
                  one by one

and marched away into a sudden tunnel.
From where I stood, I could see heel
                      following heel
                in the echoing ardour
of their single file
           my wordless goodbye
                          until

into a concealed turn
           the procession disappeared.

I hadn't moved.
           Now only one seat was still

occupied, in that guttered

hall: a stocky, mustachioed man. With a bit of caution,

he got up and gave me a pained grin. I knew his face

only from photographs: (I'd made fun
of him in a slightly evil rhyme and

                  he, angrily, had tried
to take revenge by panning my first book.)

                                  Sir,

I said, casting about for some inoffensive appellation.
I hope you see I never intended malice—I mean, so soon—

It's okay, he said, cutting me off.
                         Time evacuates intention.

(Pause.)

        But what's left, I said. Nothing! Just some cartoon
that makes the eyes fall out!

Well, well, never mind,
he replied, warming conspiratorially, fixing me in the moon
of his brow,
I guess it helped us out in the end,
both of us, didn't it?
Hehe.
Thanks.
I don't know what got
into me then, but we embraced.
I felt his forearms on
my back and I slipped my fingers through the knots
of his hair.

Okay, I continued,
that rhyme
might have been a little misjudged, but
isn't it like some

enzyme

leavening us

from within?

All grown up

a tongue between us?

Or, indeed, a mind

far enough to know

—and mourn—

4

all that was to
        and could have been
                said...?

It's teeth
        that make a single poetry, echoed he,
                looking still forlorn,
still tough.

        Anyway, they'll consign us to the lousy
depths of the database for sure,
              said I,
they'll plant the blandest gardens
            on our remains.
                And those
                  that tramp
us down
        will follow in turn

into the long
        ravine where all
            our little victories
   vanish:
        each dropped planet
              in the cry

of its jolted orbit,
        the sand of our
                languages by
                        degrees
pulverised
        and
            bleached
                into air. Well:

        we may be aught but minor poets
of the early 21st century, but
                              dammit,
we have our pride!

        Now, now, don't get scared, our dues are paid,
responded he,
        Who moves the pen
is moved by the pen.

Huh, I said.
        That's kind of a
                "labyrinthine"
           line—
                I like that!

I knew you bloody would, he said then,
This is your sort of poem, is it not?
And it's true
                    that I would have preferred
                                        to be stuck
                                                in some
febrile, living stench than over here. But listen, if this
tube-lit
        two-bit
                    indoor limbo
                            is going
                                    to be our home—
and we're trapped
            in this embrace
                        for all of eternity,

I suppose it's best
            to get comfortable. And then almost as if

our inadvertent words
            had released a spell,

            the inside became
                        the outside, a warm
breeze blew against us, fire

                        mated with air and the earth too
flung about
                        in damp clods parted
                                        to take us in.

與一位恨我的年長詩人會面

昨夜我在夢中筋疲力盡
                因為我不得不讀完
                                自己的全部作品

在一處可怖的、被翻新的螢光大廳。

這着實費了些功夫，當我完成

——沒聽到一句話，一聲喝彩——每位觀眾
都起立
                                一個接着一個

步入、消失在一處突然出現的隧道中。
從我坐的地方，可以看到腳後跟
                                        接着腳後跟
                                行走在這一路縱隊
腳步聲回響的熱忱中
                                我一直沉默的告別
                                                直到

隊列消失在
            一處隱蔽的拐角。

我沒有動。
        現在只有一個座位上

還有人，在那被熄滅的

大廳：一個敦實、留着八字鬍的男人。他有點小心翼翼地

站起身，衝我咧出一個受傷的笑容。我只是從照片裏

認識過他的面孔：（我曾用一首稍帶邪惡的韻詩
開過他玩笑，而他

　　　　　　惱怒地抨擊
我的第一本書以作報復。）

　　　　　　　　　　　　　　　　先生，

我説，從腦子裏搜出一個不怎麼冒犯的稱呼。
我希望你明白我從無惡意──我想説，很快──

他就説，沒甚麼，打斷了我的話。
　　　　　時間撤走了初衷。

（暫停。）

　　　但還剩下甚麼，我説。甚麼都沒有！只有一些卡通
能讓你眼球掉出來！

　　　　　　好吧，好吧，不要緊，
他回答道，心照不宣地緩和着氣氛，把我鎖在他的
前額之月裏，
　　　　　我猜最終是它幫助我們
　　　　　　　　　我們兩個擺脫了困境，不是麼？
　　呵呵。
　　　謝謝。
我不知道這之後
我怎麼了，但我們擁抱。
我感到他的前臂擁在
我的後背，而我的手指滑過
他的髮鬢。

　　　　　　好吧，我繼續說，
　　　那首韻詩
可能有點讓人誤會了，但
它難道不像某種

　　　　　　　酶

　　　　　　　　　　令我們倆從內部

　　　　發酵？
　　　　　　　　　　一切都在成長
　　一種我們倆人之間的語言？
　　　　　　　　　或者，真的，存在一種智慧
遠得足夠了解
　　　　——以及哀悼——

就要説的和可能已經説過的
　　　　　所有言詞……?

是牙
　　作出一首詩,他附和着我,
　　　　　　　　看起來仍然愁苦,
仍然頑固。

　　　　不管怎麼説吧,他們無疑會把我們交給
那數據庫糟糕的深潭
　　　　　　　　　　　　我説,
他們會在我們的殘渣上
　　　　　　種植最乏味的花園。
　　　　　　　　　　　　而那些
把我們踩在
　　　腳底下的人
　　　　　會魚貫而來

進入長長的
　　溝壑,在那兒
　　　　　　　我們所有的小勝利
　都不復存在:
　　　　每顆隕落的行星
　　　　　　都身處自己
受震軌道的呼嘯聲中,
　　　我們的語言

                    之沙
                        一點一點
化為塵埃
        一點一點
                消褪
                    在空氣中。好吧：

        除了二十一世紀初期的小詩人
我們可能是任何甚麼，但

                                該死的
我們有我們的驕傲！

        現在，現在，別害怕，我們應得的那份已經得到了，
他回答我說，
                那動筆的人
只是被筆在驅動。

啊，我說。
        那有點像
            「錯綜糾結」
            的線……
                        我喜歡！

我知道你傷口淌血，他接着說，
這正是你的那種詩，不是麼？
而我真是

14

　　　　寧願
　　　　　　　停在
熱烘烘的、活生生的惡臭裏，而不是站在這。但聽着，如
果這個
　　開着螢光燈
　　　　　　不值錢的
　　　　　　　　　室內靈薄獄
　　　　　　　　　　　　將會是
　　　　　　　　　　　　　　我們的家——

而我們被陷在
　　　這懷抱中
　　　　　　為了永恆一切，

我認為最好
　　　　是令自己感覺舒適。然後幾乎好似

我們粗心大意的字詞
　　　　　　　發出了一聲咒語/魅力，

　　　內部變成
　　　　　　外部，一陣溫暖的
微風迎面吹撫我們，火
　　　　　　與空氣交合，大地也
到處亂撞
　　　　帶着潮濕的土塊裂開
　　　　　　　　　接我們進去。

(曹疏影譯)

15

Short Prayer to Sound

Sound has the particular quality of being visible. It is the greater god. Vision, in evening's fog, presents a man on the cycle with his newspaper bags, the threaded breeze of his hair, even the holes of his eyes; yet, though riveting, vision knows nothing of his pain.

Sound does, for sound is pain, curled and garbled by the ganglia, stunned and suppressed, dim and thundering from some secret window. Never regular, though it may sometimes seem so. Never present, though it may seem. Rivet of moment to moment. A sack on the face with holes to see.

Imprecise, as a world seen through cloth, ease of the friend that follows. Agony internal to the shape of the amphora. The tinier holes through which a quality refines. A private lack, a riveting in some riveting act.

What does sound carry? It will not tell. It refuses to be known. So close to us, clinging, it will not tell. Mr. Subramanian wants to gather memories in its sack, as if memories in the brain's shifting imagos had actually the tangible quality of being gatherable. Alas, sound is forgetting. It has already been forgotten. It is the hole into which all knowhow disappears. The hole we can only call: *the future*.

Yet, like peas in a pod, like arguments in the agora, it follows tracks.

給聲音的短禱文

聲音有種特殊的品質，它能夠被看見。它是更偉大的神明。視覺可在傍晚的霧中，顯現一個騎自行車、帶着報紙袋的男人，穿過他的頭髮的微風，甚至眼中的孔洞；儘管這樣動人，視覺卻對他的痛苦一無所知。

而聲音能知曉，因為聲音就是痛苦。神經節將它纏繞又過濾，眩暈而壓抑，暗淡又轟鳴，從某個秘密的窗口。它從不恆定，雖然有時似乎如此。也從不呈現，雖然好像這樣。一個瞬間鉚住下一個。聲音是一只上面有洞給你觀看的袋子。

並不精準，如同透過布料看到的世界，尾隨而來的朋友的安閒，潛隱在古代雙耳瓶形狀中極度痛苦。一些更細小的孔洞，某種品質通過它們得以提煉。一種私密的匱乏，某種引人注意的行為裏那一個勁吸引人的部分。

聲音帶着甚麼？它不說。也拒絕人知道。它離我們這麼近，緊緊依附，但也不會告訴我們。薩先生想把記憶收集在聲音的袋子裏，就好像他能感知那些儲在大腦變幻不停的無意識意象裏的記憶，其實能被收集似的。唉，聲音就是遺忘。它已經被遺忘。就是那個所有技能消失於其中的孔洞。對這處孔洞我們只可稱之為：未來。

仍然，就像身處豆莢的豌豆，露天集市裏的爭論，聲音也循它自己的路徑。

（曹疏影譯）

17

Short Prayer to the Economy

prayers for fishes, tossed each to each in translucent glue
prayers for the hairier beasts, roistering in rolling tundra
if we are to conceive a world, let us conceive it—at all
    risk—one

prayers for the wily bicycle, knight of secular propulsion
prayers for uncoagulated human residue impossible to
    weigh in balance
and our economy that intricate grows, beyond
    forebearance

I've found I don't know I need I to know who can I talk to
who can I call what must I do where must I put it how can I
use it what is your number who will you call where will we
go how will we make it where will we put it who can I finger
how will they take it where is the button how can I find
it how did he get there who does he know what can it do
where does it go how do you work it what will it work take
what it will work it you do how does it where what can it
do who does he know who did he get there how did he find
it how is the button where will they take it how can I finger
who will we put it where make it how we will go where call
you what who number how how must I put where do I must
what call I can who talk to I who can to know I need I know
I don't I found I feed

18

prayers for the musical crow, the intimate mosquito, whose
    kisses are here to say
prayers for the contract killer, the contractual signer,
    unspeakable unimpeachable bond
and our shared godless theology that hooks the day to day

prayers for all projectiles, red, yellow—somewhat bluish,
    spinning inert, riskily pulsed—
prayers for gashes of quarried stone, saunas of smelted
    aluminum, ever thinning veins of copper
from where the monstrous weather grows

Feed I found I don't I know I need I know to can who I to talk
who can I call what must I do where put I must how number
who what you call where go will we how it make where it put
we will who finger I can how it take they will where button
the is how it find he did how there get he did who know he
does who do it can what where it does how do you it work
will it what take work it will what it work you do go it does
where do it can what know he does who there get he did how
it find I can how button the is where it take they will how
finger I can who it put we will where it make we will how go
we will where call you will who number your is what use I can
how put it I must where do I must what call I can who talk I
can who know to I need I know don't I found I've

prayers for the intestinal tract, whose winding road grows
  hidden
prayers for the rickety aeroplane, suspended in the air
the prickly fog will take us, will all of us be spared
prayers for every scrawny stick uncountable, each that I
  know by name
prayers for the murderous author, the deadened reader, the
  wakening good
and lastly that arithmetic not of our making, its obsolete
  fire

給經濟的短禱文

為魚們祈禱，在透明膠水裏互相翻騰
為毛髮更旺盛的野獸祈禱，在滾滾凍原上淘淘作樂
如果我們要懷想一個世界，就讓我們懷想它——面對所有
　　險境——為一個整體

為狡詐的自行車祈禱，這世俗推動力的騎士
為無法平衡、無法凝聚的人類殘渣祈禱
為我們盤根錯結生長、已越過容忍限度的經濟祈禱

我發現我不知道我需要我知道我能同誰說話我能給誰打電話
我必須做甚麼我必須把它放在哪裏我怎樣用它你的號碼是多
少你會給誰打電話我們會去哪我們怎麼幹我們把它放哪我的
手指可以觸碰誰他們如何處置它按鈕在哪我怎樣能找到它他
怎麼去那他認識誰它能做甚麼它去哪你怎麼做到的它做甚麼
使用甚麼它會開動它你做它怎樣哪裏甚麼它能做他認識誰他
帶誰去那他怎麼找到它按鈕怎麼樣他們帶它去哪我如何觸碰
誰我們放它哪裏製造它我們怎麼去在哪裏打給你甚麼誰號碼
怎樣怎樣我必須放下哪裏我必須甚麼電話我能夠誰和我說話
誰知道我需要我知道我不我找到我進食

為愛音樂的烏鴉祈禱，為親密的蚊子，它的吻就在這兒訴說
為僱傭殺手、合同簽字人祈禱，這難以言喻、無可控告的
　　繩索
為我們分享着的無神的神學祈禱，是它用一天鈎連另一天

為所有導彈祈禱，紅的，黃的——有點藍的，不帶生氣地

旋轉，冒險中搏動——
為來自採石場的石塊身上的傷口祈禱，為熔煉中的鋁的蒸
　　汽浴祈禱，為銅那越來越細薄的紋脈祈禱
怪獸天氣正從那紋脈中生長

進食我發現我不我知道我需要我知道能夠誰我說話我能給
誰打電話我必須做甚麼我必須放哪裏如何號碼誰你叫甚麼
哪裏去將我們它如何做它放哪我們將我誰觸碰我可以它如
何帶他們將哪裏按鈕是如何它找到他做如何那裏得到他做
誰知道他做誰做它能甚麼哪裏它做如何你做它可以將它甚
麼用來開動它將它開動甚麼你真的去它是這樣哪裏做它能
夠甚麼知道他做誰那裏得到他做的它怎樣找到我能夠怎樣
按鈕是哪裏帶他們將如何觸碰我能夠誰它放下我們將哪裏
它製作我們將如何去我們將哪裏電話你將誰號碼你的是甚
麼用我能夠如何放它我必須哪裏做我必須甚麼叫我能夠誰
說我能夠誰知道我需要我知道不我找到我已

為腸道祈禱，它彎彎曲曲的小路越隱越深
為搖搖晃晃、懸浮在天空中的飛機祈禱
多刺的霧會帶着我們，我們所有人都會被寬恕
為這無數嶙峋棍子中的每一根祈禱，每一根我都以名相認
為殺人的作者、麻木的讀者、正被喚醒的善祈禱
最後，為那不是我們製造的算術，為它廢掉的火焰，祈禱

（曹疏影譯）

23

Short Prayer to the Moon

Moon, though your energies be uncertain, I beseech you, protect him, protect all of us, from our nightly visions.

May the hero and the murderer withdraw gently from this, our despairing prescript.

May daylight return.

May we drink from the cup of gratitude.

May we last long enough to make note of our error.

Though burdened by knowledge, may we walk out into the open.

Though burdened by knowledge, may the clouds lift from our eyes.

Hour by hour, may we learn to free ourselves from prayer.

給月亮的短禱文

月亮，你的能量雖然無常，但我祈求你，保佑他，保佑我們
所有人，免受每晚幻覺的侵擾

願英雄和兇犯自我們令人絕望的律法中溫柔撤離。

願日光回來。

願我們取飲於感恩之杯。

願我們活得夠久，可記下自己的過失。

儘管背負知識，願我們能行至曠野。

儘管背負知識，願雲朵能自我們雙眼中升起。

時辰流逝，願我們學會從禱告中解脫自身。

(曹疏影譯)

Three Elegies for Silk Smitha

She's the slut
among white hippies on the beach,
around the campfire, hot pants
and an upright ponytail
for style; she's the dancer
in metallic feathers
and red plastic shoes. Foil
to the gangster's drink,
blackmailer's bait, the woman
you never brought home
to mother, she is
and is not
the salt of what she is.

*

At eleven I didn't know a woman's body
could be different. I didn't know
what my body could do. I watched
terrified, tranquilised. It was early
for irony. Later without yet a jot
of post-colonial theory I knew
that this was kitsch. I was leery of her
and of the Dancing Queens on TVZ
who wore tennis shoes below their skirts,
but I remembered enough to know she had it,
a shimmer, a handclap, a match's flame.

*

My last of her is borrowed too. She hangs
from the fan of a bright North Madras apartment
a thin white cotton sari wrapped
around a blouse equally white; invisible
by implication, as always was
her way. A note in Telugu says, "I
was an uneducated woman. No one
loves me." Woman
of the famous breasts and thighs and
the only seductive eyes, you were
the secret darling of Censor Board
auditoriums—capacious
and full of faces turned
from the projection's
breaching beamlight.

致Silk Smitha的三首輓歌

她是那蕩婦
在海灘上的白人嬉皮中間
圍繞着營火，很酷的熱褲
和直垂的馬尾辮；
她是那舞者
披着金屬羽毛
踩着鮮紅的塑料舞鞋。
她是銀箔，配襯大盜手中的飲料，
是敲詐者的誘餌，是你永遠不會
帶回家給媽媽看的
那種女人，她是
也不是
她所是之物的鹽。

*

十一歲，我還不知道女人的身體
可以有所不同。還不知道
自己的身體能做甚麼。我只是注視着
有些恐懼，默不作聲。要去嘲諷它們
還為時尚早。後來，一點後殖民理論
都沒用，我便明白了它們本是
矯揉庸俗之作。我懷疑她
也懷疑TVZ頻道裏的那些舞后
她們的裙子下都穿着網球鞋，
但我記得很清楚，她還有別的
一星閃光、一些掌聲、一朵火柴之焰。

*

我最後的她也來自別處。
她吊在北馬德拉斯明亮公寓的吊扇上
裹着一襲薄薄的白棉莎莉
一件同樣白的上衣；暗示我們
她不可被看透，這是她
一貫的風格。一句泰盧固語這樣説：
「我是沒受過教育的女人。
沒人愛我。」有着著名胸部
和大腿、唯一一對如此誘人的
眼睛的女人，你是
審查會議大廳的
秘密情人──那寬敞的大廳
布滿了臉孔，由
躍動着的投影光束裏
摔轉過來。

(曹疏影譯)

Thief

You, whose story
the windows tell: you're stealing
through the spider blinds unruffled. Come,

break for me the silence of these—
this room, fridge, and store-bought butter,
and the TV too, though it be lost
in electric sleep; and these cupboards
with their syntax of glass.

When you're done, come upstairs, and find,
on this desk, its solemn arrangement
of papers. Disturb them.

In the morning you have paid
a zigzag twine through the gaping front door.

I know you are there. I don't know your name.
If you come again, I will kill you.

小偷

你，窗子在講述
你的故事：正潛入
鎮靜的蜘蛛簾幕的人。來吧，

為我打破這裏的寂靜——
這房間，冰箱、買來的黃油，
還有電視，儘管它已迷失在
電之夢鄉；還有這些壁櫥
它們的玻璃秩序。

當你完事，到樓上來，在這張寫字台上
找到一疊報紙，它們
莊嚴的次序。來擾亂它們。

一整個早上，你已付出
彎彎曲曲一截細繩，穿過前門的裂隙。

我知道你就在那兒。我不知道你的名字。
如果你再來，我就殺了你。

（曹疏影譯）

Homeless Man Washing His Foot in the Bathroom of a Bus Station

(Charleston, South Carolina)

How I trail in,
desperate to decode or divine the record
that would open and end
this ancient ablution under a cold fire,
fluorescent light. How I try
and do not matter. How I'm left to depend
on irregularly regressing detail: his flared
boots worn thin,

and their flaps, twisted,
stiff at oblique angles; his jeans darkened
below the knees and corroded
in streaks; or his yellow cap
which still bore, monogrammed
in green, the cheerful hieroglyph of a former
employer. And his foot, under the tap,
unmoving, blistered,

a fat brown eel
against the porcelain; and the purple
wash of blood returning,
veins aligning, in branches under

the chipped-bark skin
of the image of the foot of this man, who
with tap water and coarse hands was trying
to make his body feel.

流浪漢在車站洗手間洗腳
（北卡羅來那州，查爾斯頓）

我是怎樣沿途跟隨
一心想破解、悟出那段記錄
它會開啟也會結束
這光管燈、冷火焰下古老的沐浴禮。我是怎樣試圖猜出
而全不在乎。我是怎樣被留給這些
斷續回放着的細節：他開裂的
靴子已磨薄

靴上的翻皮變了形，
發硬，扭扭歪歪；膝蓋以下的牛仔褲
髒得發黑，條紋處
都爛了；還有那頂黃帽子
戴在頭上，有綠色的
字母圖案，昔日老闆那興高采烈
象形文字。而他的腳在水龍頭下
保持不動，打了水皰

一條胖胖的棕色鰻魚
緊挨着瓷盆；紫色血流
在回湧
靜脈排列整齊，在皸裂樹皮般的
皮膚之下的枝椏裏
這腳的形像屬於這男人
這正試圖用自來水和粗糙雙手
令自己的身體蘇醒過來的男人。

（曹疏影譯）

34

1972年生於印度一個泰米爾家庭。曾於多個國家學習和工作，包括贊比亞、印度、南非和美國。他的詩集有《普遍的海岸》（2006）及即將出版的《蘇柏馬尼安先生》；詩作和散文都在網上廣為流傳及發行，並收錄在最近的文集如《Bloodaxe當代印度詩選》（英國Bloodaxe出版社，2008）及《新世紀語言：中東及亞洲各地當代詩選》（W. W. Norton出版社，2008）。除出版著作外，那拉揚南還發掘不同的閱讀和演繹方式；他曾嘗試把詩歌與其他形式融合，以進行科技、形體空間、動作、特定場景詩歌和與受眾溝通等實驗。那拉揚南現居於新德里，是印度註冊國際刊物和文學機構Almost Island的編輯之一。

Vivek Narayanan was born in Ranchi, India in 1972 to Tamil-speaking parents. He has lived, worked and studied in a number of countries, including Zambia, India, South Africa, and the U. S. His books of poetry include *Universal Beach* (2006) and the forthcoming *Mr. Subramanian*; his poetry and prose can be found widely online and in print, including in some recent anthologies like *The Bloodaxe Book of Contemporary Indian Poetry* (Bloodaxe, 2008), and *Language for a New Century: Contemporary Poetry from the Middle East, Asia, and Beyond* (W. W. Norton, 2008). In addition to publishing, Narayanan also explores different approaches to reading and performing; he has tried to fuse poetry with other forms in a series of collaborations, experimenting with technology, physical space, movement, site-specific poetry and audience interaction. Narayanan is currently based in New Delhi, where he is Co-editor for the India-based international journal and literary organization *Almost Island*.

出版 Publisher
香港中文大學出版社 The Chinese University Press

封面及平面設計 Cover and Graphic Designer
朱德華 Almond Chu

製稿及分色 Art Work and Colour Separation
明星鐳射分色有限公司 Star Laser Graphic Co. Ltd.

印刷 Printer
宏亞印務有限公司 Asia One Printing Ltd.

出版日期 Date of Publication
二零一一年十月 October 2011

國際書號 ISBN
978-962-996-518-1

香港國際詩歌之夜2011主辦單位
International Poetry Nights in Hong Kong 2011 Organizers

香港中文大學東亞研究中心
Centre for East Asian Studies, The Chinese University of Hong Kong

香港城市大學人文社會科學院
College of Liberal Arts and Social Sciences, City University of Hong Kong

香港科技大學人文社會科學學院
School of Humanities and Social Science,
The Hong Kong University of Science and Technology

香港國際詩歌之夜2011協辦單位
International Poetry Nights in Hong Kong 2011 Co-organizer
木刻文化出版有限公司 MUKE Publishing Limited